D1589989

LAST POEMS

LAST POEMS

by Timothy Murphy

Edited by Catherine Chandler

Fargo, North Dakota

NDSU NORTH DAKOTA STATE UNIVERSITY PRESS

Dept. 2360, P.O. Box 6050, Fargo, ND 58108-6050
www.ndsupress.org

LAST POEMS
By Timothy Murphy
Edited by Catherine Chandler

First Edition

David Bertolini, Director
Suzzanne Kelley, Publisher
Luke Hauge and Zachary Vietz, Graduate Assistants in Publishing

Cover and interior design by Deb Tanner
Cover illustration: *Marsh Grass*, woodcut by Charles Beck, reprinted here with permission of the Charles Beck family

The publication of *Last Poems* is made possible by the generous support of donors to the NDSU Press Fund and the NDSU Press Endowment Fund.

International Standard Book Number: 978-1-946163-39-4
Library of Congress Control Number: 2021940011

Printed in the United States of America

Publisher's Cataloging-in-Publication available from the Library of Congress

∞ This paper meets the requirements of ANSI/NISO Z39.48-1992
(Permanence of Paper).

Contents

AN APTITUDE FOR DREAMS

TO CLIMB ANOTHER HILL

OVER OUR WINDSWEPT LAND

TO THE CLEAR GREAT PLAINS

SECOND ENVOI

Notes and Acknowledgments

About the Author

About the Press

Index of Titles and First Lines

Editor's Note

On the morning of May 13, 2018, I received an email from my friend and mentor, Tim Murphy, asking whether I would organize his ongoing manuscript, *Last Poems*, into thematic sections. I accepted without hesitation. By the time I received his final poem, "Lonesome Dove Revisited"—which he had dictated to his brother Jim on June 17—the manuscript had grown to well over two hundred pages.

    Last Poems is a veritable *journal intime*, albeit one that Timothy Murphy wished to share with his readers. In his unmistakable voice, and often in stark language almost too painful to read, Tim chronicles his physical, spiritual, and emotional life during his final months, beginning on the day of his cancer diagnosis in early January 2018, through his various treatments, and ultimately his decision to withdraw from clinical trials—what Tim referred to as his "Mayo Moon shot."

    In Part III of "The Trial, an Ode," Tim writes:

> Good news or bad, we shall know late in June,
> two months from now. Reader, until then pray
> much as I do, not just by night but day.

> Meanwhile, I'll post all of my news to you
>   in meter and in rhyme,
>   as if I had no time.
> I don't know that I don't. I write in lieu
> of knowing you. I reach through time and space,
> hoping we'll share our Savior's radiant face.

In "Spear and Needle: The Spear," "Horseshit News, an Ode: Sacrament for the Sick," "Prayer in Deepening Drought" and "Second Envoi," Tim refers to this *posting of all of my news* as a self-imposed mission. As such, it became a sacred duty, his all-important end-of-life task, to express—with his signature plainspoken honesty and flawless craft—his deep love for family, friends, his partner Alan Sullivan (1948-2010), mentors, spiritual directors, his medical team, his gun dog Chucky, the Holy Trinity, and his beloved High Plains landscape.

Let this be my Last Will and Testament, Timothy Murphy writes in "Envoi." And so it is. Last Poems bears witness—with grace, grit, gratitude—to the life and loves of this major North American poet.

Au revoir, mon ami. Je t'aime, moi aussi.

— Catherine Chandler

ENVOI

Steve told his wife, "I think Tim's going to die,"
    ten years ago last fall,
    but answering a call
from the Spirit, I staged another try,
    a last grasp for the sky;
and so ensued a decade, far my best;
but now I must endure a cruel test

which I shall fail because my fate is sealed.
    So here's my gratitude
    for ten years' latitude
in which my crippled soul was slowly healed,
    my wounds annealed
by mercies far beyond selfish intent.
Let this be my Last Will and Testament.

WINDSHIELD
VERSES

The Sentence

Stage IV cancer? Think of it as Cat V,
the wind howling one hundred eighty knots,
raking beloved islands, casting yachts
into the trees, the handful left alive.
This is the final storm that I must weather.
Into a palm trunk drill me like a feather.

Appel aux armes

Guardian of my body and my soul,
     it's really up to you
          to see my treatment through.
St. Michael, flex your brilliant wings, control
my killers by the mercy of our Lord.
Burnish your shield. Brandish your brazen sword.

(Translation: *Call to arms*)

Three Months

I know I'm not just in the hands of God.
The Mayo Clinic has a major say.
Each doctor whom I meet there I applaud
and might survive this if he has his way.

So many gifted people there and here:
my clinic round the block, three hundred miles
to Mayo—but my truck thinks it is near,
and bears its ravaged driver wreathed in smiles,

writing his windshield verses for six hours,
both eyes fixed on the road. The fields fly by,
their snowdrifts giving way to prairie flowers.
Not yet, Lord; not yet time for me to die.

So many prayerful people to a team.
So many books of which I've yet to dream.

Fifth Chapter

Time for the Ruth and Rose and Penny show.
        To those fated to die
        so soon, my nurses try
to bring into our lives a warming glow.

Imagine life on an infusion ward,
        tending to suffering
        beyond imagining,
empathy on demand. It must be hard

to pack the sunshine in your scrubs each day
        for decades. I have heard
        many a healing word,
contagious laughter from the adjacent bay.

Add nurses to the list for whom I pray.

Ode: Three Songs for a Seraph

Luke 15:7

St. Anpiel, come once again in dream.
          I promise I won't scream,
seeing an angel standing by my bed.
          Shot through the heart or head,
legions of your beloved birds fell dead

in verses I have penned for forty years.
          I never squandered tears
for pheasant, duck, snow goose or mourning dove.
          Five Labs have earned my love.

Patron of Birds, just why did you rebel
          with Satan? Flung to Hell,
how did you find the good luck to repent?
I suppose I was seized by the same intent.
More joy in heaven? We know what St. Luke meant.

Three Plans

"Your femur is a twig ready to snap."
    So great the stabbing pain,
    I numb myself again.
I couldn't hold a puppy on my lap.

Come Tuesday, we'll connect a metal rod
    anchored near my knee cap
    (put me down for a nap)
clear to my hip bone, by the grace of God.

Radiation and chemo will begin.
    Three plans: to travel east;
    then field my favorite beast
on pheasants in the fall; to forswear sin.

Fidei defensor and my Savior's bride,
I shall have Anpiel at my side.

Plea to Anpiel

Last of my life a patch of Fentanyl?
      Oh no, say it's not so.
Anpiel, will you stand as sentinel,
      warding the ways I go
if I descend to an insensate state,
      a vegetative fate?
What need of you? Help me to climb the stairs,
      the long bridge that repairs,
restores the losses suffered through the years.
      Calmly allay my fears,
old angel friend, you have long stood your duty.
      Soon you'll reveal your beauty,
singing your treble solo in the choir
      the night that I retire.

Tuesday Dark and Early
for John Murphy

Cousin John goes to surgery with me
      while I am knocked out cold,
      my narrow gurney rolled
into the theater. The liberty

of metal implants will prove true next fall
      if I survive to hunt—
      John's little buddy runt,
striding beside a towering man, so tall

he brushes trees I couldn't dream to touch.
      My message may be grim,
      but let me honor him.
I am the sickly pigeon in his hutch.

Old Trekker

Two doctors find new scans good grounds for hope.
  The radiation beat
  it back. It's not defeat,
and in the darkness secret killers grope
to murder me, but Michael coils a rope.

So many people kneel for me. May prayer
  fly to God's listening ear.
  Let all who hold me dear
find favor with the Fates, and not despair.
I'm not yet ready for the spiral stair.

Mayo's treatment is truly cutting-edge.
  Let's see if it can save
  a trekker who could brave
pitching his tent beside a krummholz hedge,
a dizzying drop, Mount Barnard's summit ledge.

Grilled Game Dinner

Barded Bambi: bacon-wrapped venison.
      Plucked blue-winged drake, the duck.
      And pheasant breasts, worse luck!
The table groaning with its benison,

while I am sipping cream of chicken soup—
      Campbell's from the can—
      although my Chucky ran
circles round roosters on a wing-tipped loop.

"What is wrong with this picture?" Murphy asks.
      The thrill of following,
      now pain of swallowing,
tonight one of my most delightful tasks:

each guest two thousand dollars for my Press.
Time to rehearse my play list. Time to dress.

The best-laid schemes o' mice an' men

Stevie, what do I most look forward to?
       There's truth to the report
       my walks must all be short.
That has our roosters cackling in the blue.

So much depends on Mayo. If this works,
       immunotherapy
       and chemotherapy
could lay low every killer where it lurks.

Just to survive the summer I must eat,
       take Chucky for long walks
       some twenty city blocks
along the river. My return to meat,

my grilled pork tenderloin? A prayed-for treat.

Coccyx Agony

"My tailbone tries to rip right through my skin,
latest of my excruciating pains.
Punishment for some unforgiven sin?
I thought I'd got them all," Murphy complains.

Coccyx cushion. What a fabulous name.
Alliterating trochees. Did some poet
stake on this product his immortal claim
and have sheer genius enough to know it?

A U-cut through the cushion you-know-where,
so painless Murphy feels he rides on air.

Two Physicians
for Drs. Andrew Hvidston and Richard Arness

Two doctors who are not tending disease
      tend to my soul instead.
      Each hears his sonnet said,
metrical scrapings from a cornfield's leas.

The Geese will adorn a book due when I'm dead;
      they'll hang at desk or bed,
      landing or swiftly fed.
Beck and our faiths, the unifying thread.

My Knights Templar, our small City of God,
Grandpa's frame house, built by a hut of sod.

(Note: Charles Beck of Fergus Falls, MN, who died at age 94 in
September 2017, was the woodcut artist whose work appears on the
covers of Timothy Murphy's books, and sometimes within them, too.
Reference to Beck's art appears throughout *Last Poems*.)

Michael
for Kara Kapplinger

I drive under these great white waves of swans
in central Minnesota. Now black geese
in little groups launched from their clubhouse lawns
answer their great imperative: *Increase!*

Our prairie rivers haven't opened yet,
but dabbling water puddles in the swales.
Millions of years these waterfowl have met
for courtship. Now a flock of mallards sails

over a slough. How ardently in youth
I decoyed ducks and helixes of geese,
wild as these birds, oblivious to the truth:
how swiftly do our hunting seasons cease.

St. Michael, sixty years I have fared afield.
Once more lead me in battle, sword and shield.

The Trial, an Ode
for Amit Mahipal, M.D.

I.

Quickly I learn what you were going through:
    the uncomplaining pain;
    the prayers by which we gain
allies in Heaven; strength that can imbue
suffering with a meaning all its own.
Last count I had five cancers of the bone.

Alan, use all the influence you can.
    Call on the saints, and call
    angels who hold in thrall
every evil Satan inflicts on man.
If all else fails, fall at Our Lady's feet.
Have her entreat my Lord, the Paraclete,

advocate for my soul, my highest hope.
Though I'm betrothed, it's no time to elope!

II.

The trial is a go. Old Tim is in.
        Endoscopy entailed
        ultrasound, and it failed.
Not much to kill, given I am so thin.
I think my new friend Amit Mahipal
smashed through the pharma company's brick wall

for a slim sheaf of sonnets that I wrote
        and printed weeks ago,
        one for him. I know
much that I crave will never pass my throat,
and who knows if this works? Only the gods.
Always a gambling man, I'll play my odds.

Limping the Red River's flooded banks
with prayer in order I compose my thanks

III.

Today my first infusion: the immune
    system will get a boost,
      my hopes a nest to roost.
Good news or bad, we shall know late in June,
two months from now. Reader, until then pray
much as I do, not just by night but day.

Meanwhile, I'll post all of my news to you
    in meter and in rhyme,
      as if I had no time.
I don't know that I don't. I write in lieu
of knowing you. I reach through time and space,
hoping we'll share our Savior's radiant face.

Enough. I am admitted to this trial
timed to the last sweep second on my dial.

IV.

Four months, Amit declares me cancer free.
    I fear it will return
    and on my PET scan burn
in livid red. But now this liberty
from sickness will empower me to hunt
sunflowers with my wild, rambunctious runt.

Chucky, Opening Day, it's time to go!
    The mourning doves have stayed,
    cooing in fragrant shade,
the western cedar boughs that softly blow,
the junipers that roosters claw with spurs.
Here we have ears for everything that whirs.

I need my drugs so badly I could scream,
so those twelve lines were just a wishful dream.

22

V.

One look around, this is a healing place.
    Thirty-eight thousand staff
    labor to help me laugh
at sickness and despair. My haggard face

peers from a mirror, Kahler Grand Hotel,
    not where I'd choose to be,
    but my mortality
compels residence. I believe full well

if medicine can cure, I'll find it here.
    Undaunted attitude,
    a wave of gratitude
washes through one for whom death holds no fear.

Grant me a year to add to sixty-seven,
another dozen months to petition Heaven.

Kahler Grand's "Economy Room"

My sailboat berths were roomier than this.
    Stashing my chemo pump
    in bed (nary a lump),
I zone out. Now four hours of brainless bliss,

my second blast, immunotherapy.
    Amit cut by a third
    my killer's killers. Word
has reached the troops of chemotherapy

that, drip by drip, they have five days to run,
    to lay my lesions waste,
    ruin my pasta's taste.
Why can't I just kill cancer with a gun?

What's that? I need my throat, my spine, my skull?
Suffer. Amit has cells to kill and cull.

Mirror, Mirror

Necrosis: grind of dead bone on dead bone.
        I have two vertebrae,
        their disk eaten away
by cancer in my spine, a stack of stone.

Lying down, I can pop them into place
        high in my middle back
        and loud, loud is the crack.
I ask "Dear Lord, is this my state of grace?"

Two of my sisters have let slip some tears,
        seeing my haggard face,
        skeletal frame. I brace
myself to face my mirror, and my fears

resolve into resistance to despair,
ghostly visage framed by its wild red hair.

Little Lament

I've earned liver and lung
but cancers of the bone,
for what do these atone?
So strong when I was young,
now I must greet each dawn
with all that strength long gone.

Matthew 4:4

For half an hour I simply wasn't there.
I didn't sleep, because I didn't dream,
a lighted smoke fell dead beneath my chair,
I didn't torch my fingers, didn't scream,
I was just gone. Fifth time I've had a gap
in brain waves. Time to EEG a nap?

The heavy drugs and symphony of pain
flooding real sleep, all alcohol withdrawn,
this file of verse—an ever-lengthening train
ready to ship its grain out every dawn—
all make "Man does not live by bread alone"
a text from Matthew I can call my own.

Progress Report

Cancer: metastasis is everywhere,
    attacking my left thigh,
    my skull (it's aiming high),
more vertebrae. My doctors don't despair,

neither shall I. This new clinical trial
    is really my last hope,
    my drowning swimmer's rope.
I leave the Mayo Clinic with a smile,

determined Murphy will return next week
    to bolster an immune
    system that plays my tune.
Sadly, it is the Holy Grail I seek.

Thrush

Picture your mouth a giant canker sore,
      your throat once slick as silk
      confined to drinking milk,
festering lesions hurting you that score

both sides of the tongue, and then you'll know
      just what I'm going through:
      saliva that I spew
in my spittoon, foods I loved weeks ago

embittered memories, my mouthwash magic
      with every drug that numbs
      the cheeks, the tongue and gums,
keeping this side-effect from turning tragic.

Reader, pass by while trying not to gawk.
Picture a poet told he mustn't talk.

To One Who Kept Faith
for Steve Syrdal

Two weeks without even a whiff of drink?
    I think
this thrush infection torturing my mouth,
    this drouth
of longing for the agent of my curse,
    reverse
of fifty years' addiction to the booze
    comes as news
to all who feared the drink would be my end.
    Old friend,
you suffered long beside me. On that course,
    remorse
is dear. Cancer was not my chosen cure,
    to be sure.
I used to smoke three cigarettes an hour.
    The power
of nicotine to battle alcohol
    is small,
warring addictions struggling to incite
    Tim to write;
but you endured my vices through it all,
    heard the call
the Holy Spirit makes upon a true
    friend like you.

Spear and Needle, a Double Sonnet

The Spear

Spear in the spine projects its piercing pain,
    crippling my right shoulder.
    Fifteen months I soldier
 on praying. My dear acuity of brain

precludes stronger narcotics, and I think
    that I can tolerate
    this agony—force eight—
even though I've divorced myself from drink.

These last five months are certainly the best
    that I have lived, the work
    that I so rarely shirk
being home to my happiness, the test

of chemo focusing my dazzled mind
on every ode and sonnet I can find.

The Needle

I am so crazy dizzy when I stand
    bent at the waist and neck
    while husbanding the wreck
of my old body, leaving me quite unmanned.

Garage? Seems a distance, half a mile.
    Jim firmly grasps my arm,
    I wobble with alarm
those thirty paces, and I try to smile.

Mostly, though, I am grappling with my art
    practiced for fifty years.
    The needle in me steers
magnetic north, veering me far apart

from fellow men. Then comes Deliverance Day.
Now with my fellow faithful I can pray.

UNDER A
LEAFLESS WOOD

Distance

I like men who have distance in their stare,
seeming sometimes far-off as on a hill
scanning horizons where they're taking care
of herds or fields or planning their next kill,

sailors who venture far from sight of land,
climbers who summit far from the nearest town,
leaving tree line below simply to stand
nearer God's throne, the sunset on His crown

alpenglow. I have seen clouds of angel wings
lenticular or cumulus sweep peaks
in the high Rockies. For love of wind that rings
in rigging, I'm one who listens as he seeks,

who stands confronted by this cancer scare
like an old trekker greeting a grizzly bear.

Windshield Time, an Ode

First to Know

"I've never known a man
more ready to meet his end,
to wrap up his long span
and greet our Lord as friend."

So Steve three nights ago,
hearing my horrid news.
He'd walked through blowing snow,
declined the best of booze.

We've hunted thirty years,
buried many a dog.
Now as my own death nears
memories from the fog

come flooding home: God's love
descending like a dove.

Editorial Encouragement

"You have more work to do," urges Jim Babb
who made Feeney so famous in his *Gray's
    Sporting Journal,* glorious days
for Tim. Jim, lay me not yet on a slab.

To find my work honored on your back page
meant sixty thousand readers granted me,
    fellow pheasant hunters who flee
into the wild on every day the rage

for harvest drives them from some claustral town
in loaded jeeps, with Labradors in tow,
    autumn or winter's blinding snow,
to flush a cackling cock and knock him down.

Don't worry, Jim, I have Mnemosyne,
mother of muses, memory and reason.
    Cheated out of another season,
my hunting will live on long after me.

(Note: Feeney was Timothy Murphy's Labrador Retriever gun
dog prior to Chucky.)

Return to the Olson Farm

Old AA slogan, "One day at a time,"
foot in front of another plodding on,
grateful each day to glimpse another dawn,
and on my finer days meter and rhyme
conjoin to do what Tim has done before:
to probe deeply capacious memories,
to hunt once more these rows of leafless trees
where an Alberta Clipper comes to roar
and rarely does a circling eagle soar.

Hard to believe this all comes to a close,
but I thought I'd be dead at twenty-five,
and I am amazed, finding me still alive,
the ghost of Feeney weaving through these rows
of ashes, where last night's new snowdrift blows.

Windshield Time

Borne to this forty-nine-high latitude,
I've lived life on the level, the High Plains,
chip on my shoulder for an attitude,
and now I'm coping with my cancer's pains.
Anger long since gave way to gratitude,

governed emotion, thirteen years ago,
a long life freshly offered every day.
I learned to count my blessings in the snow:
to flush pheasants under these slates of grey
and write my verses when the cold winds blow;

a modicum of talent and hard work;
Alan, of course, always my greatest gift
and lift from where my worst weaknesses lurk;
(My four-by-four blasts through another drift.)
this book, a welcome task I shall not shirk.

How do I love thee? Let me count the ways,
I steal to praise the prairie I must leave.
I love our Sheyenne Valley's fiery blaze
in autumn. Just a little shall I grieve
to leave its banks where muddy waters laze.

I'll also miss December's eight hour days.
I can't recall a fall with such fierce gales
whipping a cock to safety, Chucky's craze
for pheasant flustered as away it sails,
a fall too late for me to mend my ways.

First Codicil

Time, I suppose, for Tim to dispose of guns:
two Browning side-by-sides to my friend Danny,
Patrick and Daniel Timothy, his sons,
Winnie to Steve. He'll rubber-pad her fanny
and pray St. Hubert keeps his aim uncanny.

Buck knives to junior Dan. Patrick has two
given him for his birthday at age ten,
my propane stove with which the three can brew
black coffee as the leaves blow by again,
two little boys I've loved becoming men.

Cases of ammo, Mojo dove decoys,
hats and gloves pass to the Mahli boys;
but I shall find it hard, hard to let go
of the Great Plains and months of blowing snow.

(Note: Line 4 refers to a rubber recoil pad attached to the buttstock
of a rifle or shotgun, in this case, to Tim's Winchester, or Winnie.
Tim is suggesting that Steve will need to add some length to the stock
for a better fit, based on Steve's size and arm length *vs* his.)

Murphy Mom

My news blew like a Bouncing Betty bomb,
      but now my father's bride,
      calamity in stride,
faces my likely fate with great aplomb.

I'll not suffer her age of ninety-one,
      the worries she has seen
      while reigning as our queen—
six little rug rats wrestling in the sun,

two decades when my father fell so ill,
      blood sugar, failing heart—
      and how she played her part,
her world whirling around as she stood still.

I hope this little book gives her a lift.
Strength to endure, that is my mother's gift.

St. Joseph's Cemetery

Interment, and my brother burned the sage.
      Your heart was frail so long,
      and yet your will was strong—
you lived to eighty-three, an ample age.

Black geese were calling from a pond nearby.
      Can it be eighteen years
      since daughters dabbed their tears
under that cloudless Indian summer sky?

The plenary indulgence that I earned,
      the prayer I've prayed each night
      aimed at your heavenly height,
the elegiac verses I have turned

and read to Mother by the Harvest Moon:
my gifts. Father, you'll see your son too soon.

Jimmy's Ode

Owning It

Family history is just so clean
cancer never intruded on my thought.
I've hunted hard each fall, I'm whippet lean,
but my twin vices have been dearly bought.
My brother Jim embraced a grimmer view:
"No Murphy ever drank and smoked like you."

Two Deaths, Two Generations

Jimmy is shouldering his newest role:
Head of House Murphy, I assumed with ease
two years before God drove me to my knees.
I've the support of my immortal soul
that Father lacked. Death was a font for fear.
Dog-walkers, priests, my closest friends, so near.

Worst of the Seven

On oxy I can be a space cadet.
    I'm done with distance driving
    and must confine my striving
to odes and sonnets I've not written yet.

Thank God for Jim's living three blocks away,
    putting the hammer down
    on driving out of town.
He runs my Chucky seven miles a day.

My independence, a hard thing to lose,
    Superbia or Pride
    by which Satan defied
Our Father. Salvation is hard to choose;

humility, hard to embrace as well.
Better to serve in Heaven than rule in Hell.

Fastnet, Force 10

Jimmy's "Inner Norwegian" storms to front
and center. As at the Fastnet race
Prime Minister Ted Heath's yacht swept the fleet,
Jimmy comes out of nowhere. On the hunt,
backpacking, sailing, canoeing, Jimmy's face
gives away little. As if words were sweet

treasures to be dispensed with, Jimmy's thrift
with sentences, unlike his prolix brother's,
swift to assert the first thing on my mind:
I think Jim's guardedness is a great gift,
a legacy inherited from Father's
reticence, depicted in "The Blind."

From boyhood on, Jimmy's been taciturn,
plenty of wild berserker left to burn.

The Sweetest Dream

I am the eldest of the Murphy six.
    I've always gone before
    to batter every door.
The battlements of Heaven—stone, not bricks—

towered above me in a dream last night.
    In pitch blackness I stood
    under a leafless wood,
the sky above warm with ethereal light,

angelic choristers all that I heard.
They sang, "In the beginning was the Word."

Wandering Mind

Long lines of friends come trooping through the door,
dating from boyhood or my frenzied youth.
Smiling, I tell them all the brutal truth:
they mourn my cancer, which they all abhor.

Here is a doctor; now in walks a priest,
come to anoint me with his sacred oil.
Lovers of verses honoring my toil,
they do not come to fill up on a feast

but hear these sonnets, words flung *in the teeth
of Death*, often coming twice a day,
set in the mountains where my mind can stray
and some of them set on a windswept heath:

wundswope, what a lovely Saxon word,
a kenning often thought but seldom heard.

Father Tom

We hadn't talked since Father Patrick died
       and I wrote Pat his ode,
       three songs I hope he rode
to Paradise, to laugh at Alan's side.

So good of you to call me yesterday,
       felled by your sudden stroke,
       no dog-eared Irish joke
to make *me* laugh, merely a chance to pray

in unison, much as we've often done:
       prayers for the poor who sicken,
       all who are sadly stricken,
calls to St. Michael who so roundly won

his battle for the battlements of Heaven.
Today the bread we eat will have no leaven.

Two and Five

Corporal works of mercy Two and Five:
acts of grace by my incoming friends
who check to see if I am still alive.
This damned cancer, I know well how it ends.

For their part, they are Visiting the Sick.
Drink to the Thirsty is my glad reply.
When you are dying, friendships run so thick
and prayers deepen under our prairie sky

which never seemed so cloudless and so blue,
a blessing to the ill, and so God-given.
This morning boasts a woodcut's azure hue.
I am not bitter I shall soon be riven

from friends I've treasured for so many years.
You will not watch me wasting any tears.

Two Helpers

Christian and Adam are the Shanley boys,
their laughter in my home a joyful noise.

They moved my household in the blowing snow,
lifting my spirits high five years ago.

Movers trucked furniture, but they boxed books,
bound tomes and manuscripts in dusty nooks.

Now stricken ill, I ward away despair,
hearing their carefree banter on my stair.

Annie Murphy

Annie flew from the Delaware last night.
     I've often loved to nap
     south of the Water Gap,
to wake, walk the canal path at first light,

and watch the black geese dabbling in the stream.
     From there, she likes to take
     her kayak to a lake,
raise sail and laze along as if in dream.

She reassured me that I'd find my "voice"
     some forty years ago.
     I found it in the snow,
and farming's hardships taught me to rejoice.

Lord, for these next three days grant us a blast.
We know this visit might well be our last.

Aunt Ann

You must seem quite the ancient aunt to Claire
  and Hugh. Just up the road
   to Easton, they unload
their childhood triumphs, strangers to despair
with many cuts and blisters to repair.

Think of the contrast to our own Aunt Viv,
  helpless, whom Grandma Tess
   begged Mary Queen to bless:
the sufferings with which she learned to live;
her Catholic faith all that she had to give

two tribes of children whom her brothers sent
  for babysitting. Hugh
   and Claire swim back in view,
certain their old Aunt Ann was heaven-meant
to tell ghost stories in their backyard tent,

to birdwatch in the Pennsylvania wild,
  and lead their every hike,
   repair each broken bike,
keep logs of every distance to be miled
or book devoured by such a lucky child.

Mary Katherine

Buttery scones and handmade fresh vanilla
ice cream welcomed me at my sister Mary's,
table laid out, the small deck in her garden.
      My, what a breakfast!

She had unearthed some ancient Kinko's copies,
forgotten drafts of my first two collections
which would be pruned and grown, which I'd re-title—
      a secret archive.

Greeted in uniform by my tall nephew
Jesse. Patches and badges tell his stories.
Like his brother Matthew and aging uncle,
      Jesse's an Eagle.

It was a short break, road trip back from Mayo,
tethered into the pump that drips my chemo.
Now I must study how to be a brother
      worthy my sister.

Syrdal, Ghostwriter

"Ready for an adventure." I am, Steve.
You've said Bilbo's last words on Middle-earth,
facing the Western Ocean's brilliant girth.
    Like the Firstborn shall I grieve
    to leave these lands that gave me birth?

    How many verses start or end
with quotes from you, addressed me in the field,
where we invoke St. Michael's silver shield
      to drive the dogs and send
our pheasants from the cattails they must yield?

Like Bilbo contemplating Elvenhome,
     its sunlit sands,
    I'll turn my thoughts from Rome
and set my sails for the Undying Lands.

The Manghan

Sharon has knitted me a shawl for prayer
so soft as I caress it that I stare
at swathes of color: The barley harvest there

and grass green here. The deep blue crepuscule.
Here is the pale blue of a freezing pool.
Here, sunrise under a skirt of cloud, a school

for waterfowlers crouching by a pond
where every shotgun is a wizard's wand.
The brown of camouflage that we have donned.

Its band of black, the coats of Labradors
who frolic when we free them out of doors,
and deeply sleep curled on our kitchen floors.

It wards away the chill and the despair
besetting me in this infusion chair,
for every stitch was knitted with a prayer.

(Note: A manghan, or man-ghan, is an afghan blanket or shawl with
a masculine pattern or design.)

Sleepless

Drape Sharon's afghan over blue-jeaned knees
on this chill sofa. I don't mean to freeze
this sleepless night; I hurt too much to drink
Calvados, and my random ramblings think
they can just coalesce in shapely form,
and somehow keep a shivering dreamer warm.

Dreamer? No, I am drifting out and in,
repenting decades of my heinous sin:
heresy, sin not against fellow men
but God, Whose grace I'm grasping once again
each time I flex my fingers at these keys
or pull this throw over my bony knees.

Come, Holy Ghost, quicken in me tonight
an airy dream in which I've taken flight.

AN APTITUDE
FOR DREAMS

The Splurge

On the art deco Foshay Tower's ground floor
  lay a fine French café
  famed for its *crème brûlée*
and rack of lamb, which made our spirits soar.

Couldn't afford it, but as youths we went
  to gratify our urge
  for a huge evening splurge,
and banish the dread of poverty I spent

much of my twenties with. *Bien sûr*, the cost
  would set me back a week.
  The fortune I would seek:
a paradise that's never to be lost,

but gifted; one I was designed to love—
all of our footsteps driven by a Dove.

58

Horseshit News, an Ode

Pathologist's Report

We forded Baffinland's bone-chilling streams
near an *inukshuk* marked *Le Cercle Arctique*.
Wyoming's Barnard was our loftiest peak.
I fish trout from Montana's tarns in dreams.

Past our horizon, Anegada Reef—
graveyard of inbound Spanish treasure ships.
Grilled lobster buttery on my blistered lips,
decades of sailing never came to grief.

My life already boasts sufficient length;
high adventures in the mountainous West;
serious squalls at sea, a skipper's test.
Cancer? Alan, look down, lend me your strength.

Sacrament for the Sick

Happy birthday to me —
startled at sixty-seven
and much closer to Heaven
since my pathology
result revealed the cancer —
bound for the Mayo Clinic
where my inner cynic
will seek a hopeful answer:
Can surgeons operate?
And how long shall I live?

Dear Father Paul, forgive
my small sins of commission,
my grave sin of omission,
failure to imitate
Our Lord. Let me create
more books, my lonely mission.

Good Question

My brother asked, "Are you afraid to die?"
        "Not I," was my reply,
"I'll bring *Devotions* to the Pearly Gate,
        and my forgiven state
will be sealed certain for eternity.
        I'll meet Alan, and he
will take me to King David, the new friend
        greeted at his own end;
for David led my lover's feet to Christ
        whose sacrifice we priced
beyond all treasure as we broke His bread,
        knowing we'd soon be dead.
Then I shall thank King David for the balms
offered the wounded by his Book of Psalms."

—January 10, 2018

Long Ago and Far Away

Alan forsook his old promiscuous ways
    just two years before AIDS
swept the Twin Cities. Otherwise our days
might have ended in Hades with our shades.

Sex was central to me at my age twenty
    like drugs that I outgrew
through four decades of poverty and plenty:
marijuana, mushrooms, and acid, too.

My cancer stems from alcohol abuse
    and pretty heavy smoking.
For nearly fifty years I had no use
for abstinence. I never woke up choking.

For little Pat the news last night was weighty.
I said, "You'll take me hunting when I'm eighty."

Roadside Stand

South edge of town, a roadside bonsai stand:
      Alan, you got so mad,
      (I thought that you'd be glad!)
when I showed up, my tiny tree in hand,

because a bonsai is a test of time,
      pruning for thirty years,
      watering with your tears.
You had no time. Mine was a thoughtless crime,

just one more reason to apologize;
      and love, you had no few,
      but one gift pulled you through,
my patient effort to evangelize

and buy you time for David, king of kings,
your verse translation that strides forth and sings.

Putting Back to Sea

Last night we motored, then we sailed again,
first on our *Fugle*, mammoth twin V-8s
threading the intracoastal's red/green gates,
then on our Sabre, strong seafaring men,
Alan's leukemia not lymphoma yet,
his belly not yet bloated like a ball.
Under the Tuttle Bridge we heeled the tall
top hamper of our navy sloop, and met
oncoming powerboats that yielded way.
Then we steered seaward out of Biscayne Bay.

It is about ten years since last I sailed,
not even Alan's Hobie. Memory
comes creaming back, turbulent on my lee.
I brush each headland that we ever nailed,
and dream of every mountain pass we scaled.

Poems from Pinedale, an Ode

Strophe: Cheating?

The best of nights I write verse in my dreams.
        Measures begin to drum,
        rhyme pairs start to come,
the images sequence themselves, it seems,

and when I wake I have perfect recall.
        No editing is needed
        for lines the Spirit seeded.
In gratitude I type, and that is all.

Last night the Great Divide: north of South Pass
        the alpenglow was rose
        on the Wind Rivers' snows,
the range a vast, serrated mountain mass,

Alan beside me in our Baby Benz,
our trigger fingers itching for our pens.

Antistrophe: Wyoming in Winter

Pinedale in winter? No, we never went,
        only in summertime
        to hike, to fish and climb.
Who would go for the winter storms in Lent

but Nathan Pitchford, reared by that rugged range,
        for whom I wrote an ode.
        Taking a flatland road,
he moved to North Dakota for the change.

Change is just what Alan and I pursued,
    seeking relief from drought.
    Our real problem was doubt,
the Holy Ghost the object of our feud,

a fight with God neither of us could win.
Decades later we turned our backs on sin.

Epode: War Bonnet

Big Sandy Entrance. There Cirque of the Towers,
crowned by its steepest crag, War Bonnet, glowers
    over a lake I fish,
    and two young trekkers wish
we had more time. Wyoming's treeline flowers

we've left below, a thousand feet or so,
and chimneys in the crags still hold their snow;
    but I have pitched our tent;
    cutthroats without relent
lash at my flies. No fire on which to blow,

no wood, we poach the trout on a white gas stove.
We're halfway up that crag where an eagle hove
    into two trekkers' view.
    Alan, I'm here with you.
Back to Big Sandy and our fragrant grove.

Once you've camped there, you're never really gone—
to watch the solo alpinist at dawn
    roping up for his climb
    with confidence and time
to spare—recurrent dream to draw me on.

Mountain Rescues

Two mountain rescues: high on a Cascade
a figure in a sleeping bag was roped;
    three skillful climbers coped
with a descent just opposite our glade

of lodgepole pines. On Robson's northern face,
a Bell JetRanger landed by a tent;
    the nearby schrund was meant
for no weekend hikers. Both times we'd brace

for a disaster, rescue close at hand,
nervously glassing glaciated slopes,
    offering up our hopes
to Him we didn't know or understand.

The Holy Ghost gave us a closer shave,
deciding when and where, which soul to save.

Alan's Glaciers Again

Summits we never climbed I see in dream,
     snow fields, rivers of ice
beneath the bergschrunds we bridged once, not twice.
I rise to fix the coffee with my cream,

and take a double dose of Tramadol,
     crippled when I awake
to pray for unbelieving old friends' sake
and place again my urgent morning call

to the third person of the Trinity,
     my Ghost at Pentecost
without whose intercession I am lost
just as my time zone turns to infinity.

Shopping at Publix

Bearing through life burdened with dazzling beauty,
        twelve on a scale of ten?
The Spirit didn't thrust on me that duty.
        When I was born again,

I was some decades past whatever charms
        I sported as a teen;
and fourteen years of grappling with my farms,
        likewise our orchard scene,

had left such flaccid bags under my eyes,
        "Bigger, and they could carry
groceries," said Alan, not given to lies,
        love I would never marry

not just because under the law we couldn't,
        but because we *wouldn't*.

Circadian Rhythms

I'm so wiped out I fall in bed at eight.
Then two great pains awaken me at two:
shoulder and hip. Two opioids I ate
this morning as my small world swam in view.
I've reached a state where I could use a wife
to help me through the last stage of my life.

But Alan, you've been gone nearly eight years,
swept off by cancer well ahead of me;
and dear friend, I am long since past my tears,
knowing how soon the two of us will be
reunited and reading on your cloud.
I think you listen when I read out loud.

I trust these cancer poems suit your taste.
Now back to writing, not a day to waste.

Gay Marriage

Sacramental union a priest should bless.
      What an unholy mess
our generation made of it—divorce
      often the likely course;

nearly half of all trips made to the altar
      where bow-tied grooms would falter
and many blushing brides faint dead away—
      so no, our wedding day

we would postpone, a tryst destined for Heaven.
      Waiting at sixty-seven,
I do not think I'll hear those wedding bells,
      a choir that breaks, then swells

into a wave of epiphanic song.
      I'm used to waiting long.

Feast of the Conversion, January 25

I read some sonnets at your grave today
  while earning an indulgence
  so that the Lord's refulgence
might light Kerrigan's footsteps on his way.

Today is Saul on the Damascus Road,
  Christ speaking from the sky,
  a revelation I
shared with you, love, when we laid down our load

of guilt and turned our faces to the Lord.
  Alan, greet Paul for me.
  Tell him my enmity
is gone. The Savior that we've all adored

cast Murphy down in the Damascus dust.
Scales fell from my eyes. In God we trust.

(Note: Kerrigan is poet T.S. Kerrigan who would pass away in
April 2018.)

Two Supports, a Double Sonnet

Footsore

"Tough as the leather on a Red Wing boot,"
said Steve, on Alan's tolerance for pain.
Though drugs and radiation dull his brain,
today he calls himself "A well-armed coot."
He's bought a new support, a cherry cane.

Cherry is hardwood, and the handle—bent
into a shepherd crook around the haft—
had so much heft our cancer patient laughed:
"The staff of Moses from Mount Sinai sent?
Carving and carpentry? My Savior's craft!"

Grant us the courage, Lord, to cope with loss
when strength deserts us as it drains from him.
There is a stream which every soul must swim
after it walks the Stations of the Cross.

Propped

Alan, Jimmy gave me a new cane, too,
      but mine is diamond willow.
      Propped against that pillow,
work of a whittler's knife, long time it grew

in the North Woods, arcing above the bank
      of a small brook or pond.
      Much like a wizard's wand,
it conjures cherished memories that rank

as teenage triumphs—bass on a greenwood grill,
      first fly rod, wicker creel.
      A cane? Because I feel
dizzy, far from the ground; and it's no thrill,

this fear of falling. Now I know how you felt,
propping your cane on pews in which you knelt.

Porta-Pump

Twice every hour it sips a little hit
    of poison from its bag
    which now begins to sag.
It pumps the poison, only a tiny nit

into the port implanted near my heart.
    What a technology!
    Alan's oncology
made him so sick. When not living apart

I'd slip outside to sip my secret flask
    and pray chemo went well;
    but it was always hell,
a driver's empathy my only task.

Now my lover returns that sympathy.
Alan, look down from Heaven. Pray for me.

To Msgr. Robert Laliberte

Serve my few guests the feast that doesn't fatten.
        Let them say *Kyrie*
        in Greek, and let you pray
Missa pro defunctis for me in Latin.

When Alan died, you said that poetry
        was author of his turn
        to faith, making him yearn
for higher truth, a stirring homily.

How strange we unbelievers found ourselves
        steered by the Holy Ghost,
        fed by the sacred host,
each other's books gracing each other's shelves,

his passions complementary to mine,
thrown together as if by some design.

(Note: *Missa pro defunctis*: Mass for the Departed.)

Proving Grounds

Last night we sailed Hawk Channel in a dream,
borne on the salt flow of the slow Gulf Stream.
The scene shifted; we tacked the Francis Drake,
shifted again by twenty years to Lake
Superior, round the Apostle Islands,
climax oak on their low-lying highlands.

Tyros to veterans, slowly we became
mariners worthy of that honored name.

I dreamed of mountain explorations, when
we trekked Wyoming's wilderness, young men
hiking Wind River Range, the Beartooth, too,
awestruck by each majestic montane view,
from sheared Squaretop Plateau to trout-filled streams,
with backpacks and an aptitude for dreams.

Each found the fortitude to fight despair,
to face down death in an infusion chair.

Another Aubade

Four hours of sweet, uninterrupted sleep
       happen so rarely I
       sing praises to the sky
which dimly glimmers to the east, the deep

curtain of night retreating to the west.
       I should write an aubade
       to Alan and to God.
Both lay with me, I do not know which breast

I dreamed on, but unlike the Provençal
       minstrel when he awoke,
       doves harnessed to the yoke
of dawn arising over Heaven's wall,

I have no lute to strum, no viol to bow,
only a ragged throat with which to crow.

TO CLIMB
ANOTHER HILL

Resolutions

I am determined I shall stick around
just to stick it to Social Security—
the taxes that I paid, my surety
that I stay on the right side of the ground.

I am determined that I shall not pass
but take dictation from the Holy Spirit;
and every time He whispers I shall hear it
and so remain on this side of the grass.

I confess: it is my deep desire
to work as poet for the Paraclete.
I am not ready yet to meet and greet
the other lousy tenors in His choir.

Between Slim and None

Slim just rode out of Dodge,
and I don't like my odds.
Live to defy the gods?
Furtive, the fears that lodge
deep in the stalwart heart
are never quieted.
Tonight they rioted,
frightening me. My part
is shouldering the pain,
penning a new text.
What must I take up next,
Dodge City once again?
Knowing my odds were grim
I bought a drink for Slim.

Dependency

Steve asks me, "Tim, do you like feeling stoned?"
        I answer, "Yes and no."
        This pain has got to go;
but sometimes I'm a chicken being boned,
totally different from the booze or blow.

For forty years I haven't touched cocaine,
        and now, old friend, you ask
        about this drug. I bask
in brief surcease from cancer's killing pain,
writing poems my only daily task,

save prayers I offer to the Holy Ghost.
        Maybe when summer comes
        and the woodpecker drums
on deadwood by the Red, I'll raise a toast
to the drug that leaves me lucid while it numbs.

Requited, an Ode

Muddy Boots

I've never feared I might not live till spring
which seems so far away in February;
this winter's been so long that it is scary.
Lord, how I long to see the geese take wing
from corn stubble where snowdrifts disappear;
to witness the first greening of the grass—
this year for me that might not come to pass.
Thankful I have a Higher Power to steer
my future, I take one day at a time,
write this diary, read my daily psalm
in Sullivan translation. How they calm
a hunter who so long aspired to climb
over this prairie where I sank my roots
and tracked the marshes with my muddy boots.

Requited

A month from now I hope my leg will heal
sufficiently for me to hit the brake;
snow drifts will swiftly dwindle. I shall take
a long drive to the fields where snow geese wheel,
bound for the Arctic like the natural force
they are, where far aloft the sandhill cranes
will cry *kuk kuk*, presaging April's rains.
From every hillock rivulets will course.
I shall seek quiet refuge where the Jim
River dreams of the Gulf of Mexico,
bearing its freight of soil and melted snow.
The spring goose season never called to Tim,
so I won't hunt. The hope to which I've clung
will be requited if I greet their young.

Greet the Geese

A week from now, Syrdal and I set forth
from the Red River Valley of the North
to hear three hundred thousand screaming geese
wheeling above the cornfields hunters lease.
The big water will open, and they'll come
north from their Texas marshes. Grouse will drum
on leks, dusty secrets that we can find.
In warmed topsoil, moles will be flying blind,
and pheasant cocks will crow in prairie grass
yet to green up, last autumn's beaten brass.
One hundred twenty miles southwest we'll steer
on a dear pilgrimage we make each year
to greet the geese. It is a form of prayer
by fast friends who go armed against despair.

One Block Away

Lindenwood is the park near which I live.
       This year it's turning brown
       like every lawn in town
that isn't watered. People here forgive

the flooding Red; I think it bears the brunt
       of more curses than prayers,
       for when it floods it spares
no one, and has no spillways that can shunt

water away from Fargo's massive dikes,
       which just make matters worse
       for victims prone to curse.
Sunny Sundays, half of the city's bikes

and skateboards take to pathways on its banks,
so beautiful I simply offer thanks.

Ne'er Gie the Deil His Due

I fear that I shall never see a beach
except the rocky ones at Big Floyd Lake
and Bad Axe, shores that had so much to teach
a child. This is a pilgrimage I'll take
to Minnesota's woods where I shall preach
The world is too much with us. No and no.
Dear Lord, let me outlive this blowing snow.

Detachment? I renounce the Buddhist faith
which I espoused some forty years ago.
I'm not yet quite prepared to be a wraith
or reincarnate as a famished crow,
but know that as a Scotsman *"I am laith
tae gie the Deil his due."* I look to Christ.
For me at least, one sacrifice sufficed.

Octave of Ash Wednesday

My Lenten resolution stays the same:
dimly reflect the glory of the Lord
with my small gift. Let me invoke His name,
praise His creation I have long adored.

Father, keep me alive through Eastertide
just to proclaim the Long Gospel of John
on Good Friday, two months more to abide.
I'll hear Urbi et Orbi Sunday dawn

and plunge into my favorite Book, the Acts,
where You say *Rise, Peter, kill and eat.*
Let me worship the willows' swelling bracts,
and grant your servant, Lord, his daily meat.

Though many are the sins I must repent,
I'm a confirmed carnivore in Lent.

(Note: "Urbi et Orbi" means "To the city [of Rome] and to the world,"
and is the name of the Pope's annual address and blessing on solemn
occasions, including Easter Sunday. There is a plenary indulgence
associated with receiving the blessing, even if only via radio,
television, or Internet.)

Eleven Weeks

Eleven weeks: I think they've been the best
in seven decades I have roamed the earth.
For me, work is the measure of my worth,
and chronic pain is just a cruel test.

Offer it up. I don't believe this pain
will go away, but if it lasts for years
I promise it will wring from me no tears,
but poems written on this windswept plain

whose topsoil I once farmed to my perdition.
I pray that I shall hunt again this fall,
maybe a mallard wheeling to my call,
meat for my mother's table: magic mission.

Dog Walking, an Ode

Palm Sunday

Too sick to march my Chucky in the snow,
    I snuggle in my home
    while he and Jetty roam
the riverbanks where bitter March winds blow.

Today my little friends flushed twenty deer
    and saw two eagles soar
    over the frozen shore.
One rooster flushed, crowing like Chanticleer.

Come spring (assuming that it comes this year)
    and I no longer slip
    and slide, my tender hip
has months to heal before the shotguns roar.

I've prayed for long shots I have made before.

Chucky's Army

Army of wintry walkers, lucky Chuck:
    soon you'll be flushing duck
    when the Red tops its banks
and I escort you, giving ardent thanks

that the ice breaks and the slim Bois de Sioux
    with its wide prairie view
    marries the Ottertail
to flood our valley. Here the mallards sail

with blue wings flashing to the river's edge.
      Percherons and their sledge
      are barned for summer's long
season of droning bees and robin song.

Five months, God willing, and the sharp-tailed grouse
will coax us from the confines of our house.

Best Walk Ever

Forty-foot check cord in a sunflower field
      hip-high because of drought,
      with grey doves pouring out—
the hunter's, not the farmer's, glorious yield.
Chucky, no bigger than a hunting boot,
watches Winnie to see which way I'll shoot.

First dove, and he hightails it to the Ford,
      the dove dragged by one wing.
      Precocious little thing,
he clears the tailgate as he leaps aboard
and jams a box of Milk-Bone on his head.
Grinning, the gunner heads for four-wheel Red

under the blazing blue September sky.
Whatever Chucky is, he isn't shy.

Hopes for September

Stevie and I have made a plan for fall.
    We shall take little Pat
    sporting his blaze orange hat
to Section Seventeen, and there my tall

Norwegian friend will crush the birds I miss.
    Chucky and little Jet,
    best friends the day they met,
will flush our pheasants in their frenzied bliss.

First I must fix this hip that's killing me.
    Lesions on throat and spine
    must go, and a barbed tine
on Satan's fork must fling one victim free.

St. Jude, we who are hopeless, call on thee.
Patron of lost causes, pray for me.

Next Year, Jerusalem

It is the stabs of pain that wake me up,
        my shoulder or right hip.
        I take my drugs and slip
a snack of Milk-Bone to my drowsy pup.

Sometimes I pray and just go back to sleep.
        More often, though, I work,
        delving the rhymes that lurk
in half-remembered dreams that run so deep.

Take pity on your lowly servant, Lord;
        let this cup pass from me.
        Though death will cut me free
from pain, my hand is clinging to a cord.

I've not yet sailed the Sea of Galilee
or climbed the cruel hill of Calvary.

A Scout Is . . .

A sharp stab in the lowest rib, right side,
      and I'm so paranoid
      I down an opioid
to ward away this pain I can't abide.

The headache? Cancer gnaws into my head,
      but right side of the grass
      I hope this, too, shall pass,
allowing me to write more lines instead.

Sunday? It is a day for gratitude,
      to climb another hill
      as if I were not ill,
resuscitate my Boy Scout attitude

serving so well these fifty years and five.
Day to be grateful I am still alive.

Belief in Miracles

My dreaming cheek, brushed by an angel's wing:
St. Michael can accomplish anything.

Random Thoughts on Waking

Domine, non sum dignus: how I felt
to learn so many people pray for me.
Buds swell on Chucky's baby pin oak tree
beside the kennel where his uncle dwelt

too briefly. Why must death arrive so soon
for those we love? Feeney lived twelve long years,
and now the inner helmsman in me steers
skyward two months before the year's Pink Moon

showers its petals from the heavens' height.
Long may my friends be praying for my health,
shoring my ruins with such new-found wealth.
Holy Spirit, send me a dream tonight,

three quatrains with a couplet at the close,
and send Your faithful no more April snows.

(Note: *Domine, non sum dignus*: Lord, I am not worthy.)

Let's Go Farming Again

Another week, and how this country greens.
No field work: Minnesota's in no hurry;
the Cannon River not a flood stage slurry.
Three hundred fifty miles of country scenes
fly by, and I've been put here for a reason.
For every Tim Murphy there comes a season,

and this is mine. Let's go farming again:
no drought, no debt; let's go swimming in cash
and watch the goslings hatched in April splash
into clean streams, the piglets in their pen
rolling in mud, the gift of last night's rain
that freshened all the ditches, every drain.

Two months ago I feared I'd see no spring.
Now it has come, and Tim is on the wing.

Choices

Alan, how you endured so many years
of chemotherapy defies the scope
of my imagining. My only hope
lies in a swift remission. Pray it nears.

Let me be here when frost in autumn sears
the maple groves. Let me see Chucky lope
through switchgrass. Once more *elpis* is the rope
to which I cling when fighting back my fears.

Offered swift death and an undying fame
or a long life largely devoid of blame,
Achilles chose to glorify his name.

Offered my choice, I chose to be restored
to friendship with a faith I long deplored,
to be reborn as witness to my Lord.

(Note: *elpis* [ἐλπίς] is defined as the Greek word for "hope.")

Beautiful Beacons

Few have Damascene moments. Ours were two,
both at the brink of death. The Holy Spirit
thundered, just to be certain we could hear it,
His great injunction. Two poets, simply crew

on the great sloop He sails among the stars,
we took His bearings down from every orb.
Our tasks in life were firstly to absorb
and then articulate: the planets Mars,

Saturn and Venus, Jupiter, our moon,
lamps in Heaven for His dead reckoning,
beacons beautiful in their beckoning.
Patience, Paraclete. Take me not too soon.

I need more time to magnify Your glory
and versify my very Christian story.

Spring, 2018

The flowering crabs of Fargo are in bloom.
    On east-west avenues
    just past my house, the hues
are pink and white. The honeybees will zoom

after their pollen for a week or so,
    the boulevards abuzz.
    Then black and yellow fuzz
will dive into each hive, the queens will glow

as drones perfect their domes of honeycomb,
    hexagonal the wax.
    At Orchard Glen the snacks
of bobolinks are bumblebees. The loam

our farmers seed will grow our corn and wheat;
a table set, *So I did sit and eat.*

(Note: *So I did sit and eat* is from the poem "Love (III)" by George Herbert.)

NEAR THE
MONTANE SKY

A Gift for Friends

Gratitude for my friendships is a theme
running deep in the heart of every book,
      much as a mountain stream
leaps in a dream, or trout leap to a hook.

Fast friends are few, fewer since Alan died.
He made his friends more readily than I,
      so easy when he tried
kindness to strangers near the montane sky—

our sandwiches packed in a wicker creel,
trout amandine, high Rockies' haute cuisine,
      brookies from rod and reel—
food shared with hikers in a trailside scene,
canteen Dickel offered and gladly taken,
extra crispy rashers of campfire bacon.

A Long Look Back

The best time to plant a tree is twenty years ago,
the second best, today. –Steve Syrdal

Maple Prairie and its twelve thousand trees:
      a planting of real worth
      to grace our verdant Earth
and shade the homesteads of young families;

Wilderness Camp and my three thousand pines
      from fifty years ago:
      home to the jay and crow
in winter, carven ospreys on its signs;

seven hundred apples at Orchard Glen:
      where the male bobolink
      trills when the trees turn pink.
I often dream Alan lives there again.

Something beyond these books, a legacy?
One could do worse than plant many a tree.

Plowboy Poet

Twenty feet, my green grain drill
slide-slipping round its softly contoured hill—
that's what they trusted me with at age twenty.
I don't think I'd be trusted that far still,
     for that was plenty.

My sixty horses of John Deere
  on which I'd mastered every gear
while learning how to double-slip the clutch;
landmarks on every field, for which I'd steer—
not yet, Lord, I've lost my teenage touch.

So different from my father's harnessed teams
  turning for him in dreams
  (few of them nightmares, tell the truth)
  he would not quash. It seems
all old men treasure puissance in their youth.

Sandhills Sonnet

Our revolution—tillage of the soil—
begun on April 1 at Eastertide,
built to a cresting wave: the joyful toil
of mushrooming the Sandhills that abide
in their unbroken majesty. No plough
can raise a dust storm to erase them now.

Who do we kid? We shot from drifted snow
to high desert conditions in a week
that scorched the birch rows where our mushrooms grow:
morels, the tasty morsels that we seek
in moister springs. Give thanks that the grass greens,
and make a map of future treasure scenes.

Trackless, the Sandhills' clumps of trees conceal
mushrooms that have a magic power to heal.

Friendship Seconded

I.

Down by the Buffalo a willow bends
    in an abandoned yard
    where summers we trained hard.
Long we were buddies, never such fast friends

as we became after my spirit change,
    finally coming around
    to faith I now expound
(unlikely candidate). You found it strange

I, of all people, should return to God
    from Whom you never turned.
    In your Norse heart He burned.
Hunting together mainly to applaud

Lab after Lab we whelped, hunted and buried,
    so many sides of you
    I loved (and I still do),
your *lealty* to the lady whom you married,

your reverence every Sunday we skipped church
    to quarter far afield,
    bag what the wild would yield,
weaving through trees our perching angels search

to flush pheasants, partridge and sharptails too,
    electrify the slogs
    of two delighted dogs.
Fragrances. We humans don't have a clue.

II.

Stevie, what can we hope to do this fall
    when tree rows are ablaze
      on sunny maple days
and from the corn the hungry roosters call?

If I were you, I might just hunt alone,
    no need to carry me;
      but you'll need poetry
to bear you forth and back. I can atone

for past excess with every stoic smile,
    extempore epigram,
      sandwich (Virginia ham
with Irish cheddar). Will I walk a mile?

That's all I did last year, undiagnosed,
    thinking it just old age,
      writing page after page
as cancer wormed its way into its host.

Best hope? Chucky lives out his life with me,
    his five or six more years
      in which laughter or tears
wrung from my rare readers are my fee

for a long life in which we've been best friends,
    in which we've knelt and played
      with puppies, knelt and prayed
for a good hunt. And then my story ends.

The Front Runner

N, P, and K injected down the rows,
star-bladed wheels now turning up black dirt,
poisons to punish every weed that grows;
every pest shredded, a world of hurt.

An old friend cultivates for yields of corn
beyond imagining when I was young;
truly unthinkable when I was born,
the dread-of-farming verses that were sung

in my first books—my reasonable fear,
dryland, unirrigated, prey to drought,
the new corn-boring insect-of-the-year.
My debt defeated me. I was cast out

from ten square miles of land, a memory.
My partners held it, good enough for me.

(Note: N is nitrogen, P is phosphorous, and K is potassium,
collectively fertilizer.)

Norse Dream

Muninn, Raven of Memory,
tell Huginn, Raven of Thought,
I know Valhalla waits for me,
    just as my forebears taught,

just as I know that Ragnarok
and Fenrir's ravening the wold
lie not so very long a walk
    in this subfreezing cold.

I think the Ouroboros worm
always devouring his own tail
will let the sea submerge its berm,
    and all our lands shall fail.

I shall not live to see it come,
but I'll see Odin's one-eyed face,
and I shall hear his bearskin drum
    summon me to my place.

Song of the Sibyl

Waking up from a nap
in which I wielded steel,
I take a victory lap
small as a hamster wheel.

I was full-blooded Norse,
a gale bowled from the East,
straining my sail, my course
set for an English feast.

Saxons who prate on God
don't even know his name.
By Odin are we awed;
the Sibyl won her fame

singing against all odds
the Twilight of the Gods.

The Four Hs Again
for Steve Bodio

Last night I dreamed I flew an eagle-owl,
      her wingspan just six feet,
      the talons of her feet
clutching my fist, horned ears above her cowl.

We hunted high, hardscrabble Kazakhstan,
      my barrel-chested horse
      scrambling aloft in force
for wolf, the war bird's muffled glide our plan.

The peaks above still buried deep in snow,
      we rode on broken ground,
      hunter, hawk, horse and hound
as sheep and goats lay grazing far below.

A wolf flushed far under a bergshrund's rift.
I launched. The stealthy strike was blinding swift.

Charlie Beck, a Double Sonnet

Lucky Tim's Museum

Today I bought a woodcut, *Winter Geese.*
Snow Geese is on the cover of *Fall Ploughing*
and in my *Ploughshare.* Here black geese are bowing
over the chiseled corn. A masterpiece.

Canada geese winter in Fergus Falls.
A power plant keeps the Ottertail ice-free
for "welfare geese" at perfect liberty
to skip migration. I can hear their calls

over this woodcut with its rolling land
unlike its brother, Valley cover art.
I *hear* what Charlie *sees.* It tears my heart,
Agassiz's lakeshore, its erosive sand.

Twenty-some Becks favoring every book
adorn my cottage everywhere you look.

Last Poems

Cedar homestead, a shady part of town:
here I have prairie potholes, the High Plains,
farmsteads in drifted snow, sunshine and rains,
migrating birds flushing or settling down
to feed in stubble, disked or chisel-ploughed,
and Marathon Day brings our only crowd.

Over my desk Beck's second Jesus Christ,
Ecce homo, his final masterpiece;
and now I must make room for Marsh *Grass*,
bound for this volume I have sacrificed
months in the making; and I fear the *Last
Poems* will end only when I have passed.

Charlie, we have been partners all these years.
We'll laugh together when this book appears.

The Timothy Murphy Collection

"Best collection of Beck in private hands,"
       my old friend Charlie said;
       but after I am dead?
Dispersal? All my siblings took their stands:

retain the woodcuts, perpetuity
       of public access. Thus
       they'll never see a fuss
amongst themselves. Their unanimity

stunned me, resolved a major source of stress.
       Silkworms, withhold my shroud—
       I've never been more proud
of five siblings who voted to address

our prairie's need to keep these works together
       for showings in small towns,
       gems for Carnegie's crowns.
My heart feels lighter than a pheasant's feather.

Master and Mentor
for Richard Wilbur

Man shall not live by bread alone,
    but by God's every word
    that ever children heard.
Moses strikes water from a stone,

manna falls from a cloudless sky;
    but these are merely signs
    of God's deeper designs
targeting us. Five decades I

envied my Master, old and wise,
    who wielded faith I lacked,
    whose distance vision tracked
the circuits of our Maker's skies:

Richard Wilbur, towering friend
I'll follow to my blessed end.

Little Ode for Syrdal

March 17, 2018

Amateur Hour, I called St. Patrick's Day
        as well as New Year's Eve.
            Steve, you would not believe
how many drunks will weave their bleary way
to package stores, then, three sheets to the wind,
drive off oblivious to how they've sinned.

Now looking back, thank God those days are past;
            nobody on the road
            at risk of being mowed
flat by a fool Eugene O'Neill could cast
as Irish moron in a tragedy.
Now I'm a pro. These days my strategy

is get a tiny buzz on every day,
then sober up two hours before I pray.

"Being a Guy"

"As fun at five as over fifty-five,
            best part of growing old,"
            Steve chops ice in the cold,
draining my glacial walk. No man alive

ever prayed harder for my threatened soul.
            Syrdal is close to God.
            Rightfully overawed,
he prays that with these punches I can roll,
            bob, and weave.
            Thank you, Steve.

Syrdal Speaks

Steve speaks in a dream,
likely a smoky bar:
"Things aren't all that they seem;
though Murphy's come so far
and the known risk is grim,
I'll stack my chips on Tim."

Then Steve adds with a grin,
       "All in."

Cobbler, stick to thy last
for T.S. Kerrigan (1939–2018)

All wheels to Minneapolis: move that grain,
then roll cars in their thousands back again
from Cargill's giant riverside depots
to ship more corn before November's snows.
Shift fracking sands to fracture Bakken rock,
proof of our revolution, such a shock
to western North Dakota, long so broke
under the Jim Hill Railway's iron yoke,
more coal than any strong young man could stoke.

Tom as an editor could make me grow,
to free myself from barbed wire in the snow
swirling forever round our landless pole,
where *Ursus maritimus* cubs still roll
under a green aurora's ghostly glow.

Five Editors

Editors in their wagons circle camp.
I owe a weighty gratitude to these,
        eager tonight to seize
more readers. Drawn by my flickering lamp,

my gatekeepers, many; but there are five
who bet their reputations, took a chance.
        With each of them I'll dance.
They broke trail for my readership, alive

for decades in some cases. They believed
in the nobody I was and still would be,
        loving the wilds in me,
placing faith in each bird Chucky retrieved.

Tonight I'll stroll the Valley's riverbanks
with five to whom I owe my deepest thanks.

Lament for the Small Presses

I hate to see an indie press go down.
     It's happened to me twice,
     and Lord, once would suffice:
the wind farms whirling all round Washburn town,
     a summer's epic flood,
     creditors sniffing blood,
our replica Fort Mandan left to drown.

The NDSU Press feels just like home.
     Soils of the high coteau
     forever prone to blow,
have blown me back to my Svea-Bearden loam,
     whose farmers haven't shirked
     to fund us as I've worked.
Here let me stay, never again to roam.

Starstruck

Three miles down Constitution Avenue,
I passed Twain's house in Hartford, took my place
upon a park bench, Capitol in view,
hoping in Stevens' memory to erase
narrow prairie perspective. On that bench
Stevens held a paint brush, not a wrench.

A quarter mile further, Heritage House,
the Frost Garden, I traveled to soak up,
imbibe that genius, dragging my sober spouse,
this young man in a hurry, starveling pup
who played Frost's readings from the West Side Y,
envying Frost so cruelly I could cry.

My closet liquor store across the lane
lay where I sipped Jack Daniel's in a shower
(the world's greatest depressant), and the pain
of my inferiority had power
to spur my efforts to surmount such doubt.
On this spot, Frost and Stevens duked it out.

The Davis Dreams, an Ode

Prayer for the Sixth of June

On what fresh blessing shall I spend
my feeble power of the page?
It's growing stronger as I age,
so I treasure each hour I wend
my long way to a promised end.

Chucky, it's less than ninety days
till Opener. I know some bins
where doves confess their little sins
of theft. "Let's hope a silver haze
bedazzles them," a hunter prays.

First, I must relearn to stride
and overcome this dizziness,
to pause each summer day and bless
my prospects for an autumn ride
with you, your crippled gunner's pride.

Uncle and Nephew

Feeney was five and Murphy fifty-five.
    No pheasant cock alive
but trembled when we two took to the field;
    and what a glorious yield
of upland game a dozen years ago
    from first leaf drop to snow.

Chucky, I fear the only thing you do
    better than him is cue
your face into a toothy grin, and pose
    for close-ups when it blows,
that and the way in which you nap and pray
    Sunday and every day.

Feeney was such a pagan—every hill
or slough, his first commandment, "Thou shalt kill."

Blessings at Midnight

Three poems today, they are no livelihood,
just kisses for the cross of olive wood
      Maurice gave Ellen. "Gift
      this cross to Tim. The rift

cleaving his heart needs healing more than yours."
It's midnight, and a passing storm front pours
      blessings on every farm,
      dispelling my alarm

that drought would bake our seed beds. Now I pray
that blackened sunflower heads will come in play
      in just three months; that man
      and dog will make a plan

to pass-shoot mourning doves on Opening Day
from a fine field of Aastad-Hamerly clay.

The Davis Dreams

Chucky, alas, no Davis Ranch this year,
      where Feeney tried to teach
      grouse. It's beyond my reach—
fifteen sections where stalking herons spear
pike from the prairie ponds that I revere.

Turds bleach around the skulls of every cow.
      Cross-fenced for grazing,
      with strings of cattle lazing,
that ranch reeks of prehistory, not now,
its sixty quarters virgin to the plough.

So many years of hard-earned memories,
      there I get lost in dreams;
      and every time it seems
the only landmarks are its forty trees,
good places to get down on muddy knees.

Lonesome Dove Revisited

For thirty years Syrdal and Murphy rode
trails, each looking to the other's need;
the Black Labrador was their only breed,
each of them lightening the other's load.

Before and after every arduous outing
they knelt together, no daylight between
them on matters of faith, as I've often seen.
In dove season Murphy did all the scouting;

Steve was the senior partner in pheasant season,
far better long shot and better horseman.
Murphy was small, Syrdal a towering Norseman,
Murphy the faster snap-shot, stands to reason.

Hip fractured, riddled with cancer, nearly dead—
"By God, Hell of a party!" Murphy said.

OVER OUR
WINDSWEPT
LAND

The Sky Is His

The birds are His, not ours—
whether the hawk that flies
so freely in the skies
or pheasant cock that cowers
in the deep prairie grass
where Chucky longs to pass.

The sky is His, not ours—
however hard I try
I shall not learn to fly,
fledging the eagle's powers,
spiraling in the blue,
banking and dazzling you.

The grass is His, not ours—
and the wild prairie rose?
In the west wind it blows,
and by His will it flowers,
each ward of earth and sky
reflected in His eye.

The Burn

Salvation can proceed from holy places:
      the vista of a peak
      Alan and I would seek;
rainbows over Tortola during races;

the glow of cognac (after pheasant chases)
      at the Schwab's Paradise,
      or from some stranger's eyes;
serenity that beams from certain faces.

Prefiguring or following the turn
      to Christ whom we adore,
      it lights the sinner's core—
surely the Holy Spirit's ardent burn.

Prayer to Charlotte Wilbur

Your death day, Holy Tuesday, Charlee, pray
      hard for your "young" friend
      facing a painful end,
chemo and radiation. Day by day

I trudge to treatment, trailing my slender hope,
      wishing only to write.
      Burdened, I wake at night
weighed by an anchor eye-spliced to a rope,

symbol of *elpis*. *Pistis, agape* too,
      with these must I surround
      my soul and stand my ground,
trying to die unbowed. I pray to you,

much cherished matron in the Heavenly Host.
Put in a warm word with the Holy Ghost.

(Note: *Pistis, elpis, agape* refer to St. Paul's faith, hope
and love.)

Maundy Thursday

I dream the Lord is washing my vile feet,
    and modesty enjoins
      the cloth around his loins.
Red wine to drink, with bread and oil to eat,

my Savior now blesses and breaks the bread,
    "Do this in memory."
      I know tomorrow He
suffers his torture. Crucified, then dead,

he leaves His parting gift, the Eucharist,
    to sinners such as I
      who contemplate and cry
for our unworthiness. Then I, dismissed

the Presence in this Thursday dream, repent
and count my blessings at the close of Lent.

Good Friday

To Father Thomas O'Dwyer

My best Good Fridays I've read John with you.
The Holy City's sky was black and blue:

the Son of God, the perfect sacrifice
for Whom the Roman soldiers cast their dice.

His life was flawless and His ending grim,
that we might share eternal life with Him.

Easter Vigil

The Vigil and the past year's pedal tone;
    our candles in the dark;
    a Gospel from St. Mark;
an angel comes to wheel away the stone.

In his unbloodied linen blazing white,
    Christ comes from the gloom.
    Roll, rock, from the tomb,
I wrote some years ago. The Marys' fright

gives way to worship. The Apostles' *Acts*
    will guide us, all next week,
    who have not far to seek,
who love these legends that we take as facts,

and find our faith in these two thousand years.
Go, legionaries. Rack your rusty spears.

Spiritual Directors, an Ode

I.

All loved a broken Scout
alcohol had done in.
God would forgive my sin,
and slowly draw me from the depths of doubt.

II.

When Howie does a laying on of hands,
my torn shoulder gets better for two days.
What do we have in common? Eagle Scouts.
But unlike Howie, I've lived on the outs,
gay, alcoholic. Friend, he understands
the Holy Spirit and His healing blaze.
You know that you've been prayed for when he prays.

Though I had scarcely seen him after college,
I sought him first, when first the Spirit struck,
he tucked me under the shadow of his wing—
me, who made such a hash of everything.
Widely revered for his deep Bible knowledge,
he saw a seeker with a streak of pluck.
Much that I lack I can make up in luck.

III.

The Holy Spirit took me by the hand
as though I were a frail ten-year-old boy
      bearing a spark of joy
      I didn't understand.
All memory of that blessed week is blurred,
for I had just been kidnapped by the Word.

He bid that my Directors steer my feet
in full detox—a drill I thought I knew,
      they had the clearer view,
      the sea change I'd repeat
in a heartbeat. I tell it once again,
a dire example to succeeding men

who, like me, need the mercy of Our Lord.
When born again, my future was restored.

Different Ministries

Why do I pray for every priest?
Because he has a hard war in the world
　and wages battle with the Beast.
On Sundays he must see our thoughts are whirled

upward by homiletics. Damning none,
he must cajole and comfort such as me,
urging us toward the Father's only Son.
　Bless me Father, I longed to be

　a priest when very young,
searching my conscience and the Father's will.
　When all the hymns were sung
I found the priesthood just too tall a hill.

Domine, non sum dignus, I confessed
and turned my efforts toward a different test.

(Note: *Domine, non sum dignus*: See note on poem
Sed tantum dic verbo.)

April 27, 2014

Titan or giant, you bestrode our world,
     and only under you
     could we return, we two.
I cheered the papal banners they unfurled

at Peter's Square on St. Faustina's Day,
     cheered with your pilgrim Poles
     the *Missa* that consoles
a flock after their shepherd's gone away.

I heard the Santo subito! they cried.
     This month, as I renew
     the faith restored by you,
Let me cast off *Superbia*, my pride,

on the vile midden of my waste regrets.
This is the month for clearing all my debts.

Pentecostal Ode

Vigil of Pentecost

I'll rise at three to see them broadcast live
      from St. Peter's in Rome
      clear to my humble home.
Into Acts 2 I'll take my yearly dive,

a mighty wind rushing about the house,
      a cloven tongue of fire
      marking my deep desire.
Our early Church becomes our Savior's spouse.

Then comes "In the beginning was the Word,"
      the first chapter of John
      I'll read in Greek at dawn.
Tomorrow sacred ashes must be stirred

six weeks after the rock rolled from the bier
to fire my faith up for another year.

Flood Times in Fargo

Pentecost and our orchard's blooming peak
       would often coincide
       and we would host with pride
parties. We knew not what or Whom to seek,
for we were pilgrims by the heavens crossed,
poets without the gift of Pentecost.

I think the Spirit wanted us to spend
       long decades in the dark
       miles wide of the mark,
each seeker clueless to the promised end,
the rainbow of God's covenant to man
given to Noah. Then *our* floods began,

recurrent nightmares, refugees driven forth
by the heartless Red River of the North.

Dream Time on Pentecost

Alan, come to me in dream.
Poach these trout beside a stream
tumbling from the snows above.

Finish them with olive oil,
lemon pepper, hungry toil.
Do this as an act of love.

Be my helmsman, seize the wheel,
steer us past the reefs that steal
thunder from incoming waves.

Pick for us from road cut rocks
proofs of earth's primeval shocks.
All we know is Jesus saves,

we are found who once were lost.
Come to me this Pentecost.

Pentecost with Maurice

Spiritual Director

I kiss your tiny cross of olive wood
       maybe ten times a day,
       and God sees it is good,
Creation. Every time I kneel to pray,

I thank you for your firm and loving hand
       guiding me, very lost
       over our windswept land,
fumbling footsteps to my first Pentecost.

Surprised and pleased that I had come to God,
       you taught that Jesus' love
       didn't require the awed
poet who is directed by a Dove

be worthy of the sacrifice Christ made.
God gave us every olive in his glade.

Very Holy Couple

Maurice, your cross is transformed to a token,
      an emblem of great power
      I turn to every hour.
My spirit, not my body, is unbroken,

and this, its whittled haft, becomes a key
      with which I can unlock
      at all hours of the clock
all Three, the Persons of the Trinity.

Ellen tells me you spoke inside her head,
      urging she make this gift.
      You landed me; adrift,
I kissed keel at the Tiber. Now you're dead

she claims you two grow closer every day.
Look down on me from Heaven, friend, and pray.

Trinity Kiss

Maurice, I give your cross my Trinity kiss,
      the foot and either hand,
stigmata borne by saints who die in bliss.
      Francis will understand,
the saint and not the Pope who rules in Rome
where many sinful prelates make their home.

When you greet Alan, tell him about your cross
      and Ellen's precious gift
I celebrate. It ransomed every loss,
      gave me an hourly lift,
and it has turned you to a nightly muse
as I unburden me of cancer news.

What it will make me, friend, I cannot say;
but it's a wondrous cross on which to pray.

An Examined Life

When people's prayers for you run really deep
it gives new meaning to the depth of debt
I tallied once in dollars when the threat
of bankruptcy troubled me in my sleep.
When friends pray, it is different. They ask God
to lend life to a man with slender hope.
Barely controlled I slalom down this slope.
Looking back on my decades, I am awed
to contemplate the narrow scrapes I've had
   from youthful idiocy
   and insobriety,
behavior worse or worst, or merely bad.
Tectonic was my shift in attitude,
the path from greed and wrath to gratitude.

The Last Gospel

ἐν ἀρχῇ ἦν ὁ λόγος

Words of the Holy Spirit, make me listen,
for all my inspiration comes from You.
Dew on the green prairie grass, you glisten;
from you I grasp my most expansive view.
Truest of texts mankind has ever heard,
John wrote *In the beginning was the Word*,

then, *God so loved the world, He gave His Son.*
The Last Gospel closes the Latin Mass.
By this let every day I have begun
and every prayer I breathe at evening pass;
the Gospel Acclamation of my choice,
it fires me with the ardor to rejoice.

Wake me for comfort after I have dreamed:
You are put here on earth to be redeemed.

TO THE CLEAR
GREAT PLAINS

Matthew 25:1

Like a wise virgin
let me light my lamp to meet You.
Let hope take root and burgeon
in my sorry heart to greet You.

Fourth of March, 2018

for Francis Xavier McCarthy

I.

Thirteen years back this very day I bent
      before the Trinity—
      decades of heresy
and all my modest fortune wildly spent.

Hitting bottom, I thought it at the time:
      confused, depressed and lost.
      Ten weeks from Pentecost,
the Holy Spirit spun me like a dime

and snatched me from the grasp of suicide.
      He marched me up a path
      leading from drunken wrath
to the clear Great Plains air where I abide,

trying to craft a Christian way to live.
Murphy is the first I must forgive.

II.

I know firsthand it's a hard hill to climb.
    Now I approach its end
    way too early, friend.
Cancer catches me running out of time,

a final lesson in humility,
    in long-suffering pain,
    washing life down the drain.
Fishers of men have their nobility.

I wish I'd studied more than these few years,
    Sts. Matthew, Luke and John,
    St. Mark, his stories drawn
sitting at Peter's feet, the Roman spears

ranked around Christ and cross at Calvary:
Eli, Eli, lama sabachthani?

(Note: Eli, Eli, lama sabachthani: Christ's utterance from
the Cross: "My God, my God, why hast Thou forsaken me?"
First line of David's Psalm 22.)

III.

Benedict sent a vision, and you called,
      the saint and not our Pope
      Emeritus, a rope
of *elpis* grasped on which our Savior hauled.

You claimed, "Jesus loves drunks and faggots, too,"
      and I laid by my gun.
      The early springtime sun
streamed through my glass wall with its river view.

Francis, we'd fallen silent thirty years.
      Thank God you tracked me down,
      thank God you *talked* me down,
for that day death was least among my fears;

I, who hadn't the least clue how to pray.
Had you not called, I couldn't write today.

Act of Contrition, a Daydream
for Fr. Paul Duchschere

Headwinds of death blow fiercely from the North
          as I sail forth
to meet them. Tailwinds lulled me to sleep,
          cruising the deep
Drake Passage. Bring it on, a Christmas wind!

          Father, I've sinned.
My last confession was a week ago.

    And now our fresh, new-fallen snow
has quite wiped clean the filthy slate of winter.
          Take the splinter
out of my eye, dear Father, feel my pain.

          Behold the plain
stretching before us, nothing but barbed wire—
the boundaries of which I never tire.

(Notes: Fr. Paul Duchschere is the pastor of Saints Anne
and Joachim Catholic Church in Fargo, ND. Christmas
wind refers to an easterly trade wind that becomes stronger
and remains moderately strong for a period of at least
several days during the period from early December through
mid January.)

Je m'accuse

I do not blame my God.
This bed that I have made
wearies me. I shall nod
in shame when I'm a shade:

smoking and drinking, both
risk factors, present, past;
many a broken oath
to quit that didn't last.

To the approach of spring,
to wagers no one wins,
faith, hope, and love I bring.
Forgive me for my sins.

(Note: *Je m'accuse: I accuse myself [of the following sins]*
is a phrase uttered by the penitent in the Roman Catholic
Rite of Confession.)

St. John's University and Abbey

Each time I stop, Francis, I pray for you,
knowing your faith suffers its latest test;
this Breuer Chapel with its hilltop view
a place of healing where I pray my best.

Benedict, I'm unworthy of your Rule.
Yours was the vision sent that saved my soul;
your abbey soars, so let me go to school
and live a life of quiet self-control.

Benedict, pour your blessings on my friend
who was your vessel fourteen years ago.
Francis, I'm ready now to make an end:
call Shadrach, Meshach, and Abednego.

Nebuchadnezzar, I am in your hands.
Here is the furnace. Here my angel stands.

(Note: Tim is referring to his friend, Father Francis Xavier
McCarthy, to whom he dedicated the poem "Fourth of
March, 2018." Benedict's Rule refers to *Regula Benedicti*, a
book of precepts written by Saint Benedict of Nursia. Lines
12–14: see the Book of Daniel 3:19–26.)

Farm Boy

Places I'll never see? The list is long,
beginning with Jerusalem and Rome.
My grounding on the prairie was too strong,
too firmly fastened to our Bearden loam—

this challenging but goodly place to farm,
where seven decades I have struggled now,
where long I skated close to grievous harm,
and farrowed many a Large White Landrace sow.

It rooted me the windsweep of the Plains,
where I can only guess how the balance tips,
prey to the randomness of patchy rains
and certain Horsemen of the Apocalypse,—

a small Antaeus, standing on his land,
whose gravity I've grown to understand.

(Note: The great strength of the half-giant Antaeus, the Greek
and Berber mythological figure, depended upon his constant
contact with the Earth.)

Montane View

At every visit from a loving friend:
"How many times will I see him again,"
    I ask, "before my end?"
I've not been truly close to many men.

Too many of those few are long since gone.
Now it becomes my time to follow them,
    twig from the great tree sawn,
a sprig of scion wood, a slender stem.

Soon I shall leave behind my wealth—my verse,
sonnets drawn from the Rockies' snowy slopes
    where I climbed to rehearse
my distant death, terminus of my hopes,

    the earthly ones. We are immortal, too,
and heaven surely dwarfs a montane view.

Little Prayer

You do not know the day,
you do not know the hour,
I quoted. Now I'll play
with my diminished power
and see our melting snow
flow to the Arctic sea,
come spring, before I go
to earthly nullity.

My anger I regret.
I think it leaves no trace,
though I feel guilty yet.
When I behold Your face,
dear Lord, lift my head high.
I am prepared to die.

(Note: Citation is from Matthew 25:13.)

Prayer for the Farmers

Tonight I add a fourth chapter to prayer.
I pray first for the ministries of priests
who serve me at our sacramental feasts
and showed a way back from my black despair.

I pray next for the sick, for I am one,
an aging man with a badly injured shoulder
who hopped so nimbly once boulder to boulder,
though thank God I can still shoulder a gun.

Third, for my worthy friends who knew not God;
I pray they've passed the Gates. Arriving thence,
may they behold Christ's radiant countenance.
On seeing angels, may they all be awed.

Fourth, I shall pray that every farmer thrives,
beginning with the five audacious Millers,
masterful farmers all and skillful tillers
of land the Lord leases them for their lives.

As usual, I route these prayers through Mary.
This death sentence I have received from cancer—
to which doctors and shamans have no answer—
is a small, final cross that I must carry.

Each of us has a roughshod race to run.
Care for us, Lord, and let Thy will be done.

Prayer in Deepening Drought

With each five days on this infusion pump,
        every one of my pains
        searches out new domains.
Wielding my diamond willow cane, I stump

vertiginous, lost in my oxy cloud.
        Sonnets and odes I write
        but sleep little at night.
Silkworms aren't knitting up my shroud,

for I shall be cremated when I'm gone
        to lie at Alan's side,
        each one of us a bride
of Christ. Today, an hour before the dawn,

I pray not for surcease of Murphy pain,
but for my farmers. Send a two-inch rain.

Scant Relief

"On the just," says the Lord,
but I choose not to judge.
Limping these days, I trudge
the earth I long adored
before turning to Christ
whose sacrifice sufficed
to save my sorry soul.
This oxycodone haze
gentles my painful days,
and gingerly I roll
off of my couch. A rain
blesses our browning plain—
an inch? More like a third.
Prayers in a drought were heard.

(Note: Citation is from Matthew 5:45.)

Reply to the Dean

Death, be not proud—
noblest of sonnets.
When said out loud,
followed by minutes'
defiant thought,
in boyhood taught
much about death
in one pure exhalation of the breath.

Death, thou shalt die.
No, Dr. Donne,
that will be I.
My race is run,
timed by the sky,
your *Busie old foole, unruly Sunne,*
and timed, too, by the indifferent moon,
to end so soon.

So Hard to Do, a Double Sonnet

Custom Gunworks

To me, what does a fine craftsman inspire?
Confidence. Check the volumes on his shop shelf.
The fake is someone too full of himself.
Today I write for an old friend, Kevin Hayer.

Check out his eyes, the fit of his tool belt,
let it sling low. Simpler the business card,
the better, calloused hands from working hard,
happiest filling the inside straight he's dealt.

Two billionaires needed your tiny lot,
corner of University. Retire?
I hope many young craftsmen will aspire
to earn the modest fortune that you've got.

All we've ever wanted to do was hunt;
now I'm happy to lay me down a bunt.

So Hard to Do

Gunsmith like windswept has a Saxon ring.
      Bring you a crippled gun,
      and I'd be on the run
long before mourning doves were on the wing.

Stuck safety? Just remove the slender slide,
      spray with some exudate
      of magic, let it wait,
and the next morning mount up for a ride.

Your mom tells mine your shop dog's been put down.
      Kevin, so hard to do,
      the ashes that you strew!
Bear them far from the bounds of Regent town,

some pheasant covert under a cloudless sky.
Read him these lines. Tim Murphy says goodbye.

Holy Cross Cemetery

No to my family. I shall lie with him,
a new country graveyard, young maple trees
and spruces that he loved, two Seraphim
adoring Mary. There, on grass-stained knees,

I pray not for the sake of Alan's soul.
King David saw to that. I ask that he
speak to our Lord, all fates in His control.
Alan, look down from Heaven. Pray for me.

There shall we lie, insensate to the wind
that scours the prairie so incessantly,
the two of us, redeemed, who gravely sinned
but turned our faces to the Trinity.

Only our ashes, though. No skeletal bones.
Poet I have engraved on both our stones.

SECOND
ENVOI

A mystery to them, our fervent selves:
     as soon as we are born
     to Christ we earn the scorn
of some who keep no Bibles on their shelves.

Yet we are called, go forth, evangelize;
     and I have a large flock
     milling round Peter's rock.
Far larger than my Diocese, its size

I pray will swell long after I am gone.
     Go, little book, and sing
     till all who call Christ King
from every corner of the earth be drawn.

A mission carried out in measured rhyme?
I know no finer way to spend my time.

Notes and Acknowledgments

The editor wishes to thank and to acknowledge the following persons for their invaluable input on many of the poems in this volume: Rhina P. Espaillat, William Carpenter, and Jennifer Reeser who, along with the editor, comprised a close-knit group of readers Tim referred to as his "Committee Members" with whom he communicated on a nearly daily basis in the winter and spring of 2017–2018; and to Julie Ann Sih, not only for her exceptional labor of love in proofreading these poems, but also for her insights, critiques, and suggestions with respect to many of the poems themselves.

The following poems, sometimes in different versions, were previously published, or are forthcoming, in these journals:

The Alabama Literary Review: "Envoi," "The Sentence," "Return to the Olson Farm," "The Four Hs Again," "Farm Boy," "Next Year," "Jerusalem," and "Montane View"

Commonweal: "Friendship Seconded"

First Things: "Prayer for the Farmers"

Gray's Sporting Journal: "First to Know"

The Hudson Review: "Distance"

Modern Age: "Fourth of March, 2018"

About the Author

Timothy Murphy (January 10, 1951–June 30, 2018) is known as a major American poet who lived on the Great Plains. He was a fascinating and complicated man, a child of North Dakota, who wrote deceptively simple poetry. He had been a grain and hog farmer and an insurance man, but the twin joys of his life were poetry and hunting. His last years were spent in a quiet life in a modest cottage in Fargo, North Dakota, where he wrote poetry full time, even when he was hunting pheasants with his faithful dog Chucky.

Although his poetry explores universal themes of faith, family, spirituality, farming, friendship, love, and death, it is all profoundly rooted in place—the Red and Sheyenne River watersheds, in North Dakota, on the Great Plains, at the heart of the continent. Somehow all of it tries to make sense of the wind-swept northern plains, exploring how place shapes poetry and how poetry shapes one's experience of place. Murphy's poetry, like grain and grass, grows from this place.

Murphy grew up in the Red River Valley of the North. After he graduated from Yale College as a Scholar of the House in Poetry in 1972, he farmed and hunted in the Dakotas. His memoir in verse and prose, *Set the Ploughshare Deep*, was published by Ohio University Press in 2002. With his partner, Allan Sullivan (who preceded him in death), he translated *Beowulf*, which AB Longman published in 2004. His previously published collections of poetry are:

- *The Deed of Gift* (Story Line Press 1998)
- *Very far North* (Waywiser Press 2002)
- *Mortal Stakes | Faint Thunder* (The Dakota Institute Press 2011)

- *Hunter's Log* (The Dakota Institute Press 2011)
- *Devotions* (North Dakota State University Press 2017)
- *Hunter's Log: Volumes II & III* (North Dakota State University Press 2019)
- *Hiking All Night* (North Dakota State University Press 2021)

About the Press

North Dakota State University Press (NDSU Press) exists to stimulate and coordinate interdisciplinary regional scholarship. These regions include the Red River Valley, the state of North Dakota, the plains of North America (comprising both the Great Plains of the United States and the prairies of Canada), and comparable regions of other continents. We publish peer reviewed regional scholarship shaped by national and international events and comparative studies.

Neither topic nor discipline limits the scope of NDSU Press publications. We consider manuscripts in any field of learning. We define our scope, however, by a regional focus in accord with the press's mission. Generally, works published by NDSU Press address regional life directly, as the subject of study. Such works contribute to scholarly knowledge of region (that is, discovery of new knowledge) or to public consciousness of region (that is, dissemination of information, or interpretation of regional experience). Where regions abroad are treated, either for comparison or because of ties to those North American regions of primary concern to the press, the linkages are made plain. For nearly three-quarters of a century, NDSU Press has published substantial trade books, but the line of publications is not limited to that genre. We also publish textbooks (at any level), reference books, anthologies, reprints, papers, proceedings, and monographs. The press also considers works of poetry or fiction, provided they are established regional classics or they promise to assume landmark or reference status for the region. We select biographical or autobiographical works carefully for their prospective contribution to regional knowledge and culture. All publications, in whatever genre, are of such quality and substance as to embellish the imprint of NDSU Press.

Our name changed to North Dakota State University Press in January 2016. Prior to that, and since 1950, we published as the North Dakota Institute for Regional Studies Press. We continue to operate under the umbrella of the North Dakota Institute for Regional Studies, located at North Dakota State University.

NDSU NORTH DAKOTA STATE
UNIVERSITY PRESS

Index of Titles and First Lines